Houndstooth

Also by John Lowe
Lines Between Virginia and John Lowe
(Melbourne Poets Union, Union Poets Series, Chapbook #27)

John Lowe
Houndstooth

Acknowledgements

Some of these poems have been published previously:
'The Island' in *Blast*, no. 13, 2010
'Rock' in *Australia Poetry Collaboration*, no. 20, 2013 (online)
'Fern House Statues' and 'Horse and Wagtail', 'The Crystal Coach'
in *Wand'ring Steps*, ed. Brian Edwards, Mattoid/Grange, 2015
'Shore' and 'Whale Watchers' in *That Untravelled World*,
ed. Brian Edwards, Mattoid/Grange, 2014

My thanks to Linda Weste, Vicky Tsaconas, Cecilia Morris,
Les Wicks, James Walton and all participants in their poetry
workshops, especially my wife Virginia

Houndstooth
ISBN 978 1 76109 079 0
Copyright © text John Lowe 2021
Cover image: Emmie Norfolk from Pixabay

First published 2021 by
GINNINDERRA PRESS
PO Box 3461 Port Adelaide 5015 Australia
www.ginninderrapress.com.au

Contents

Thermal Region	7
Wrecking Yard	8
Cello Under the Chin	9
Optometrist's Waiting Room	10
The Island	11
Country Graveyard	12
Black and White	13
Rock	14
White Wall	15
Cat and Bricks	16
Fern House Statues	18
Hiroshima	19
Crete	22
Horse and Wagtail	23
Oleander	24
Moth	25
Circular Quay Sunday	26
The Crystal Coach	27
Festival at Myangle	28
The Ice Palace	30
Shore	32
Beach Walk	33
Seagulls	34
Whale Watchers	35
Night Plane	36
Strangler Fig	37
New Year's Eve	38
Traffic Island	39
Night Driver	40
Smoke	41

Houndstooth 42
Roman Museum and Cathedral 43

Thermal Region

New Zealand

We leave the lawns, the formal gardens,
to look on nature free from polite restraint;
it belches, spits and farts without decorum,
hinting at the underside of everything.
A fine skin lies on fiery powers,
our world of lawns a veneer on hell.

The roughneck earth can hurl a city down.

What else does the boorish bully offer?
Golden terraces, a chartreuse lake,
cones of frost born of furnaces,
a pool of interplaying jade and topaz.

Beauty springs from lack of shame.

Wrecking Yard

Style and motion no longer matter:
destruction's silent aftermath abides
in twisted guts and broken bones of steel,
torn metallic nerves and plastic tissue,
the only touch of nature flakes of mud.

Picnics, dealings and deliveries,
lovers' meetings, shopping trips
should not have been so violated
and so become memorial. Apparent now
are anger at best, fear, pain, oblivion,
plain implications of a crushed door.

'You're in luck, mate, we've got your model.'
Rejoining electronic veins and arteries,
the skilled mechanic with deft fingers
effects the transplant of the part.

I drive out past a line of bodies,
compilation of follies and of errors,
like a shelf of history books.

I join the smooth road, yet again
enabled by another's sacrifice.

Cello Under the Chin

Everyone has a cello
fixed beneath the chin
and holds an obligatory bow.
All are set to play.

Some never reach the bridge,
else scarcely scrape beyond,
or cannot finger a string.

Others make bumbling murmurs,
randomly grumble and buzz,
but most perhaps can rise
to a humble simple tune.

A few will make a melody
sublime, transcendent, soaring
over admiration, over envy.

Optometrist's Waiting Room

On either side
the walls are covered
with ranks and files and rows,
a spectacle of frames.

Whichever way I look,
they keep a faceless silent watch
with no brains behind.

I am the centre of attention.

Am I some 'beloved' leader,
king of the unthinking,
national charlatan,
an emperor lacking clothes?

Or am I one
condemned by the emperor,
stared down by a multitude,
outcast, untouchable, leper,
refugee?

The eye chart will not spell out
an answer.

The Island

Rising and falling in expectation,
passengers strive to scan the sea,
vying to spot the island lying ahead.

They have slipped the bonds of land,
its bends and lashings, knots and bindings,
to cross the narrows of their wishing.

Closure is the goal, the easy grasp,
as if within the binding of a novel –
the promise of their travel, set against
the continental openness of history.

Bound to the island, the prow is stirring
the froth of desire, mixing in a faith,
for if there are utopias,
islands too must be, to hold them.

Burrs and thorns are in the wool,
the fungus and the spore are on the boot,
the virus on the skin. The past is pandemic
and incurable. There are no islands.

Country Graveyard

Forebears and heirs are here coeval.

For time still clings like clay
in living loves and hates,
or quick in the darkness of ink.

Contemporary respect, retrospective contempt –
however remembered, each one bears distinction
till the last emotion has sunk into the earth.

A generation inherits fired casts of mind,
brickbats, and the shards of ostracism.

This is not a final place, but one of continuity.
Past and present constantly pass the torch to future,
having lit the fuse.

People die as they have lived,
in fits and starts, in more or less,
as one by one they join
a vast, discoloured, cracked mosaic.

Here in the sun children leap from grave to grave.

Black and White

The rubbish tip is a tower of rejection, a Babel,
and there on the lowest level
a black pond lies, flat ooze and slime
swart from the trash,
ultimate swamp,
sump of the sump.

And wading there are the whitest birds,
gulls,
like priests in albs.

With all of the air as their heritage
and all the foam of the ocean,
have they sold their birthright
for a cesspool?

Extremities shock and delight us,
as sure as black makes white
and virtue, vice.

For the world is a mixing of purities,
where pure contaminates pure,
and humans,
each in a tangled uniqueness,
seek for an essence.

Standing up on the shards of Babel,
I silently hail the birds
in fellowship.

Rock

Sailors once again engage
that old thug god, the sea,
boiling and bullying.

Above its boundlessness
stands the lighthouse,
built upon rock to avoid.

The navigator,
rocking upon the sea,
can now draw a line
that walks the water.

The lighthouse
offers deliverance,
a place, a fixing –
upright, whited,
it stands upon its bluff.

White Wall

I see upon a broad white wall
a rough pale grey patch.
Someone with a spray can
for a brain has trumpeted
'I vandalise therefore I am.'
Another has tried expunging
but their colour does not match.
The war on graffiti is just,
but whiteness still is spoiled.
If Rorschach, the great muse,
should ask me, I would reply
'No victory will ever be complete.'

Cat and Bricks

Making a path,
I take solid bricks,
set them stolid in the ground,
and the light, lithe, quicksilver cat comes
and walks upon the work.

I consider colour, texture, contrast,
as he flows against my ankle,
senses the brick I next require,
and sits on it.

Curious at the changes in his garden,
he stares at me,
with soft meow to reassert
the old feline exchange
of fealty and lordship.

Puss, a brick on the paw
would not be pleasant, besides
you're in the way.
Push off, Puss.

Piss off, Puss!

He winds against me again,
accepts my perfunctory pat,
retires to sit and watch wide-eyed,
from time to time
quizzically moving an ear.

What are more opposite
than a brick and a liquid cat?
In spite of patterns and textures,
it is cats that I prefer.

But there is a time for bricks,
and a time for cats.

Fern House Statues

In the fernery innocent maidens face
a soldier unsheathing a sword.

Our forebears were right to place
marble next to fern,
things so unlike
that they belong together,
one white, so dense,
the other greenness forming into feather,
in and of the air between.

The white and the green,
two worlds, beget a third,
the joy of contrast.

A visitor may turn from strife,
from partisans assailing mind and heart,
may pause, enjoy a fruitful opposition,
then, sword in hand, depart.

Hiroshima

It seems an ordinary street.
The sign – *The hypocentre* –
is sudden, startling.

No learning is needed to grasp the meaning:
the arcane word plucks the passer-by
as powerfully as any mariner.

*

When goodness goes out into the world,
to seek any goal
it wades through the sump of the world,
and cannot survive unsullied.

Joshua drew not his hand back…
until he had utterly destroyed
all the inhabitants of Ai.

*

In Japanese *ai* is *love*.

*

After heat beyond all knowing
the thirsty drank the black rain of death
for the first time in the world.
Orphans cried down unconsoling streets,
Ai ai ai…

*

Maple trees leafing –
the Peace Memorial Park,
verdant canopies.

A school group dedicates a chain
of paper cranes to be laid up
behind glass in many colours.
Youth, life, colour, love,
here are so enhanced:
Ai ai ai

*

The Museum:
A thousand books about a war
are not as eloquent
as a crumpled school satchel.

A young Australian boy
caricatured Japanese troops
stopped by a blast, beset
by diggers crying 'At 'em, boys!'
then took his bag to school.
People of Hiroshima,
please forgive me.

*

Schoolgirls come.
They smile, they laugh,
say they are feeling hungry.
This is refreshment.

Let them grow,
put forth their leaves,
their flowers,
fruits of all kinds –
the many branching plants of love.

Ai ai ai.

Elsewhere
kimonos in a museum tell
of lava beneath Mount Fuji.

Crete

This is a place of invasions.

The Venetians and Turks
came and went,
and Crete was re-created.

I stand, a rank-and-file tourist,
on grass graced with purple flowers
dispersed against the green.
I look down to see them close.
Paterson's curse –
Mediterranean beauty, bane of Australia.
I admire, cattle sicken, horses die.

My uncle stood here earlier,
waiting, rifle in hand.
He saw buds opening in the sky,
white blooms against the blue
without beauty – parachutes,
parasites, infesting the land.
Crete bled once again.

A prisoner, he was taken
where food had bacteria
invading and ulcerating.
This curse he took to Australia,
to marriage, family, business,
in pain, until the day
death came from within.

Horse and Wagtail

Grazing grass with tear and crunch, Horse slowly advances,
Wagtail springing, flittering, close to its jaws.
The huge companion rouses up a midge,
and Wagtail bounces in, snatching opportunity.
The lordly, leisurely diner tolerates the perky gobbler,
but once or twice raises his head, 'Too close, my friend,'
and Wagtail springs away, returning nevertheless
in feathery dauntlessness.

Here is chestnut dignity and latent power
and by its jowl is pirouetting cheek,
both with the gift of beauty.
What then is beauty?

Oleander

Among old suburban weeds
a small oleander languishes,
scraggy stems barely hinting
at humid air or tropical moons
or brilliant days of beaches.

It stands a distant cousin
to Van Gogh's creamy nodes and spikes
clustering, thrusting across the canvas,
by art enhanced.

Here it offers all it can afford,
bitty flowers to beautify the world,
and more than once it hears the words
beware, avoid and poisonous.

Moth

The blackness of the midnight room
extends through the window,
expands through the universe.

A fluttering tells
of a suffering moth
caught in a web unseen.

Light years of unfeeling black
connect it to the stars.

Circular Quay Sunday

Salty harbour breezes
yield to fumes of kerosene;
the firestick juggler balances high,
the player on the didgeridoo
punctuating continuity.

Alexander ferries its ancient name
from fleets before the First,
commuting weekday sentences,
and sorbet eaters stroll, to sobs and throbs
punctuating continuity.

Gelato, gyros, sweet and sour, are offered
to lemon blouses, hijabs, slip-on scuffs.
Bradfield stands in stolid boots,
with Utzon vaulting in grand jeté,
the ground bass accompaniment
punctuating continuity.

Ferries sail and buses roll,
people saunter, as if the saw
to seize the day were over-energetic.
Deeper than Sydney Cove, the didgeridoo
against the rumble of the trains
is punctuating continuity.

The Crystal Coach

The crystal coach is rolling through the bush.
Timber splitters pause and look, and bend
back to work, for this is jailer country,
where all must heave and hew, on pain of death.
A drover's wife peers through bars of bark
and thinks of necklaces and vases and survival.
The crystal coach is drawn by unicorns
beyond the bounds surveyors have prescribed,
beyond the fencers setting posts and rails.
Some may not see the unicorns till sleep
has freed them from their levels and their lines.
Dreams evaporate like pools in drought.
Others will be blessed with power to conjure
unicorns and coaches at their will,
and cherish within themselves another thing
than iron pots, splinters, dirt and sweat.

Festival at Myangle

The woolshed posts are structural changes
from balladeering staves of yesterday.
The evening speaker carefully arranges
her notes upon a ribboned bale of hay,
sizing up the customary flock
of weaners, comebacks, old merino stock.

> Out on the board Professor Dagboy stands,
> grasping his chardonnay in thick pudgy hands.

The lambswool secretary patters through the herd
to where he ramifies the conversation;
she taps his arm, he leers, but given word
to mount the dais, the hub of acclamation,
he broadly beams, obeys the soft behest
to say some words of greeting to the guest.

> With Sony's patent speakers fixed
> and denim cuffs pulled back,
> to introduce the VIP
> he sets off down the track.

Far from ignoble strife of madding youth
Dagboy turns the shed into his college,
feels his voice come velvety and smooth,
as from the golden fleeces of his knowledge
he picks the crimps his listeners expect,
theme and form politically correct.

       The speaker waiting in a cane-bottomed chair
       notes well the glazing of the eyes everywhere.

He reaches anticlimax, then deflates,
the audience applauds the change in agenda.
Ghosts of owners, ringers, scabs and mates
squat together out on the dark veranda,
perplexed by Dagboy's endless woolly thread,
astounded at the women in the shed.

       Beyond, a darker spirit howls, in tears
       for vanished territory and tribes and years.

The Ice Palace

The ice palace vanished long ago
it is said,
but who cannot visit it at will,
who has the will?

I think therefore I can walk,
I think therefore I must walk
its zero corridors
within embalming walls
where skeletons have no cupboards.

For what is transparent
is there and is not there;
parts melt at partial rates,
reshaping at random.

Melted from line and square,
its old design turns to curves,
and stalactites of stalag concentration.

What escape?
Down crackling crevasses,
every one a fractal palace?
Down, into palace after palace
of frigid passages, stalagmitic bars,
the ribcages of old memory?

Climb then, climb the bars,
like a clown up a greasy pole,
or a submarine survivor
in an artificial bubble.

Again I breathe the green light of day,
and mourn the part of me I left behind.

Shore

The shore is ceremonial:
earth and water meet and salute.

One lays on the beach gifts from out of its vastness,
the other offers granules,
millions, aeons in the making.

Scattered wrack and shattered shells
do not lack beauty, even in decay,
lying between the promise of a hinterland
and the far mystery of unseen places.

Coves and capes, headlands and bays,
celebrate their difference by embracing.

Hand in hand we walk through sand and water,
partaking in the portent, the keen potential,
of a border.

Beach Walk

The sea retreats over heel-sinking sand,
briefly we tread hard floor of beach,
then down again, toes, heels, into wet yielding.

Here the beach and the ocean meet
to make their ageless trick of three:
soft, hard, soft – why so? We stop,
refill our store of talk, debate
the fleeting firmness in between
a million grains of sand and sea's infinity.

We each propound, write sayings in the sand
(both aware), enjoying
the lesson of the morning, each to each.

And having taken in the learning,
all the learning of one saying,
each of each,
hand firm in hand, we walk again
between the clouds, the foaming and the sand.

Seagulls

A crumb falls,
and a bush telegraph of gulls
runs along the shore.
They flap and squawk,
converging, contentious,
white as lawyers' linen,
grey as theologians' robes,
yellow as gold.

They stand impatient
or pace demanding,
arching and ruffling necks,
krawking and quarrelling.

Throw a crumb,
create a frenzy
of squabbily flapping,
law, war and trade
confounded in feathered confusion.

The pageant deifies the picnicker,
who deigns to answer invocation
like Discord at the feast,
choosing when and where to start a skirmish,
from up there in the gods,
watching and writing the play.

Crumbs are transient; their bestower
must resign the godhead and depart:
the birds pace in cold disappointment,
the higher being leaves the empty ground.

Whale Watchers

A brief community facing the ocean
stands in vigil up upon the verge,
seeking in the surging element
the power and the intelligence of the sea.

Stranger speaks to stranger, debating
the chances of a manifestation.
Random glances, binocular quartering,
neither yields a sighting.

They hope for tonnage hurled into the air,
gravity defied by joyful gravity,
for mountainous children frolicking,
miraculous fountains rising.

They will not hear the language of the whales,
but know that there, out in the turbulent grey,
deep calls to deep. Land creatures, they know
only the rumble and thunder of the surf:
imagination suffices here for wonder.

Throughout the day watchers turn
and leave this edging of the elements.
They have sought, but have not seen,
epiphany from the other domain.

A mariner seeks in vain to sight a beacon.

Night Plane

A community of chat and smiling crew
rides a void of astronomical black.
In the pit of pitch beneath
there comes a patch of crossing lines of light,
an ideogram –
a word of Confucian wisdom,
or Tao enlightenment out of the abyss?
Uninitiated, I see only
a country town, community
of chat and smiling locals.
The lines are short. Streets end,
engulfed within unending night.

Strangler Fig

A soaring bird brings a seed in dung
up to a giant that properly aims
to thrust up through the canopy above.

The seed gains its niche and sends
tendrils descending, begetting
a hundred vampire descendants.

Binding and winding downward,
the filigree assassins devour
the lifeblood of a stolid tree.
The giant within succumbs,
leaving a woven shell.

The fig cannot escape its lot
of taking on its victim's shape.

New Year's Eve

The long wounded monster writhes in its final throes,
swollen and smelling of gangrene and of roses,
with an unsupportable load of grief and delight,
it drags toward merciful midnight and relief.

Congas are forming,
corks are popping
and people are raising
glasses, paying
lip service at least to hope.
And there is kissing,
Juliet – Judas –
and there will be dancing,
until the strokes of midnight
knock away another piece of ground.

The old year sinks exhausted on the earth;
thousands join in Auld Lang Syne
to celebrate another Hydra's birth.

Traffic Island

Like other strangers to this city
I know the directions roughly,
feet weighted by slight doubts.

I wait on this island, exiled
within an exile city.

On either side
the local vehicles' velocity
of confidence confidence confidence
whooshes and swishes the air.

The drivers are driven by goals,
the fuel of familiarity,
green lights and confidence,
confidence confidence confidence.

The lights change,
the humble pedestrian sheds one exile,
and takes again his tentative way.

When drivers at their destinations stop
and step human from their cars,
do they divest themselves of knowingness?
And walk uncertainly
in a far from wholly known world?

Night Driver

If the driver has a goal,
the road is a teasing friend,
providing means
with tedious bends and hills.

Headlights, required companions,
carve out of night a domain
too solid for fantasy,
too fluid for possession.

The lights of town and house imply,
callously, connections of the day,
and warm lovers sleeping.

And so he drives to end the flow of night,
he drives to reach
solidity, love and rest.

And if the driver has no goal…

Smoke

On the horizon white smoke rises, sending
the national scent of crackling eucalypt,
acrid nostalgia of boiling billies,
long afternoons of burning off,
close and cosy evenings
since hearthstones were here in the land.

What is beyond the hill?
The hating, hated red core of heat,
battlers engulfed by agony,
homes reduced to hearthstones.

A reader looks up from an old romance,
sniffing the air.

Houndstooth

Some say a chessboard
shows that life mixes
good and bad, joy and pain.
But surely
the interpenetrating complexities of houndstooth
portray it better.
Black will violate white
and white will find a way into black,
the struggle never ending.

Roman Museum and Cathedral

Köln

Behind the milestones, deities and monuments
a narrow length of window runs,
lens to a later time, displaying
a sample of the Dom, its statuary and buttresses,
a slice of massive beauty.

A thousand years or more apart,
sculptors shaped their brotherhood of skill
to lusty demigods or virginal saints,
in alchemy transmuting stone
to flowing robes and personality.

Apprentice grew to master
as hammer, chisel, hand and brain,
all became a oneness,
with stone a countervailing friend
resisting, then resulting
in Minerva or Madonna.

The Roman and the journeyman
looked on their finished work
and on the vision in their heart,
and felt the artist's ageless discontent.

www.ingramcontent.com/pod-product-compliance
Lightning Source LLC
Chambersburg PA
CBHW070051120526
44589CB00034B/1984